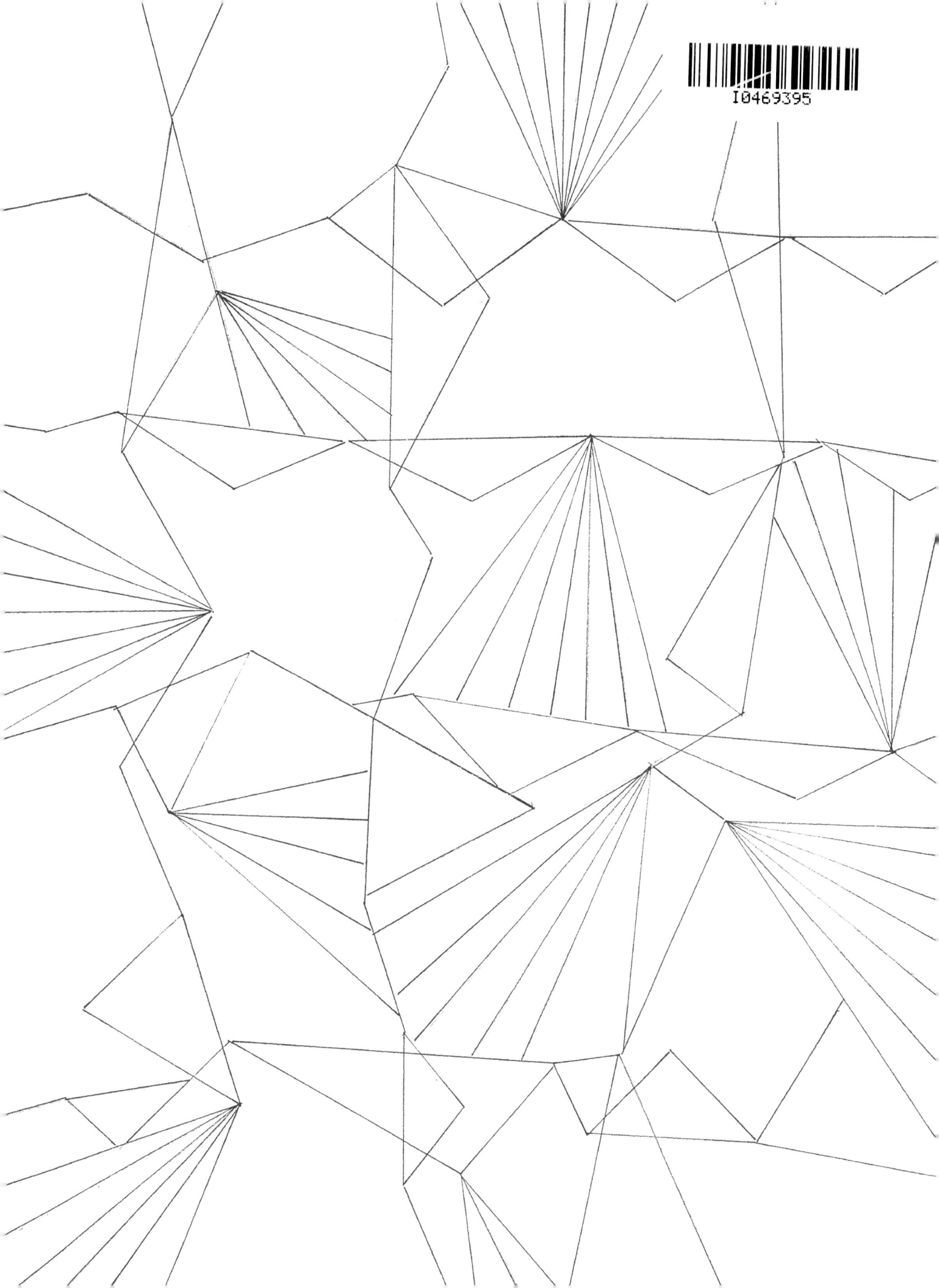

Writing in a journal is an effective tool for use in the healing process.

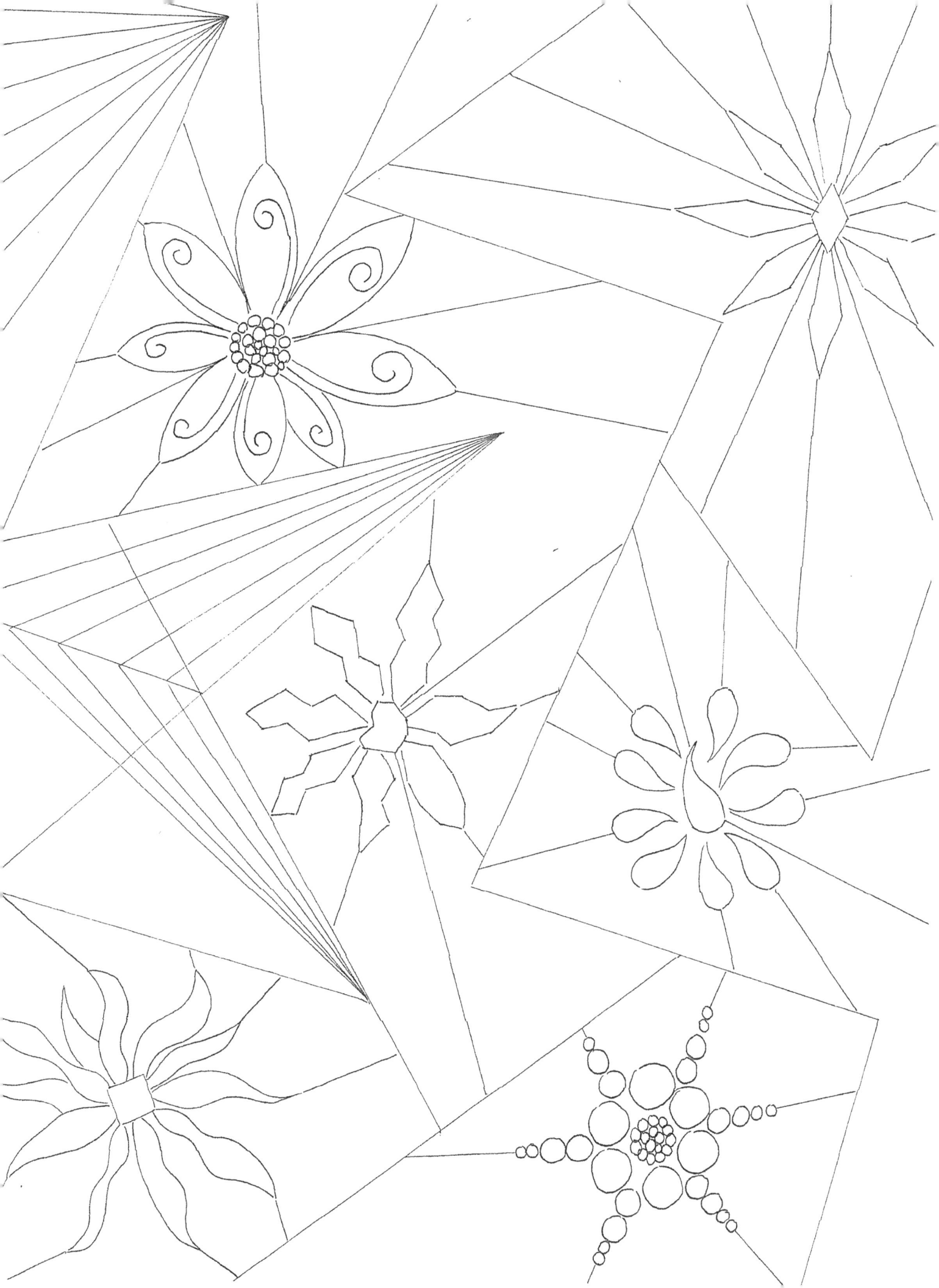

Journaling can be about gratitude, things that really matter to you.

_____

_____

_____

_____

_____

_____

_____

_____

_____

_____

_____

_____

_____

_____

_____

_____

_____

_____

_____

_____

_____

_____

_____

_____

_____

_____

_____

_____

_____

_____

_____

_____

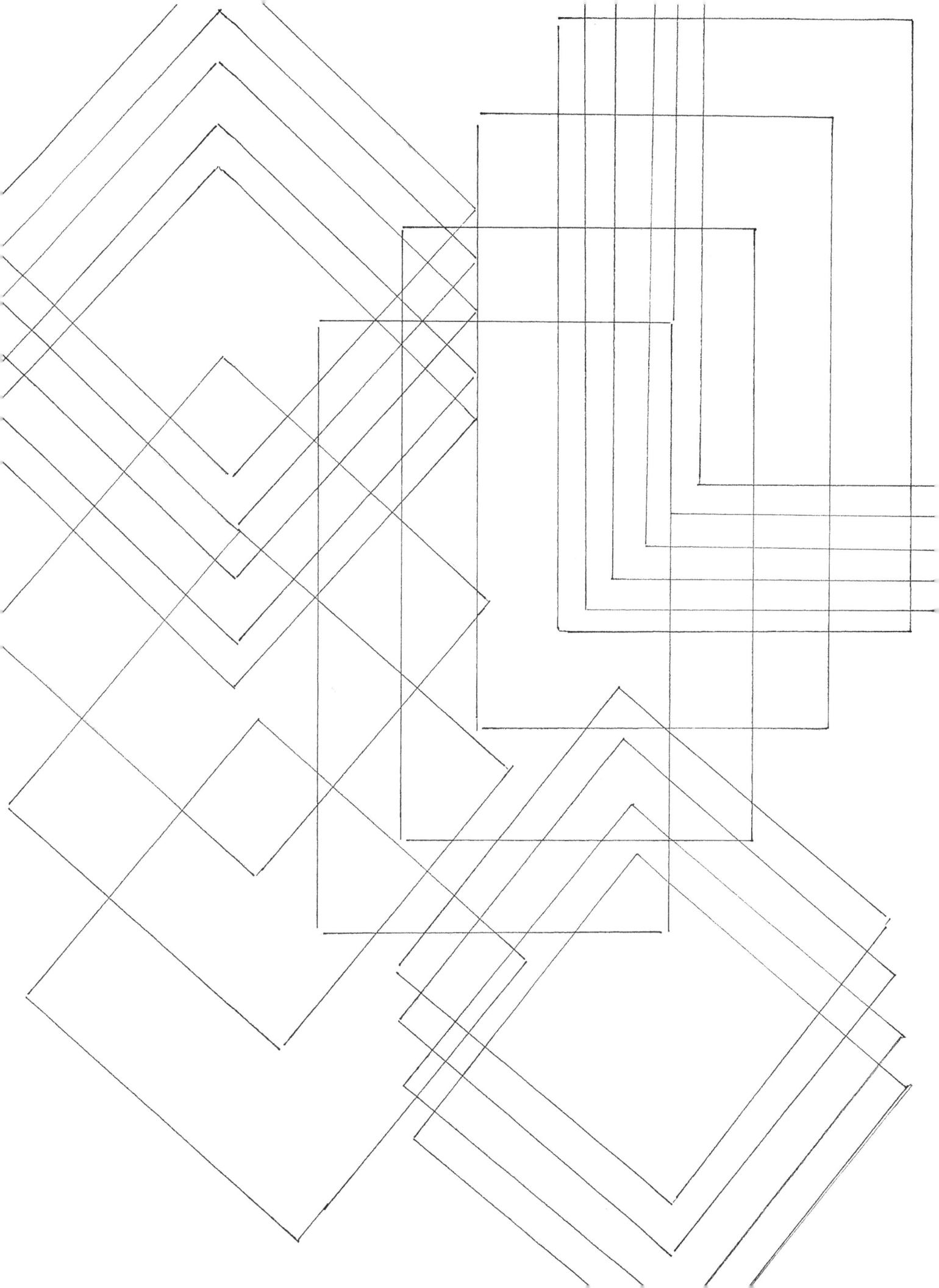

Journaling is a form of meditation. It helps you relax and become quiet.

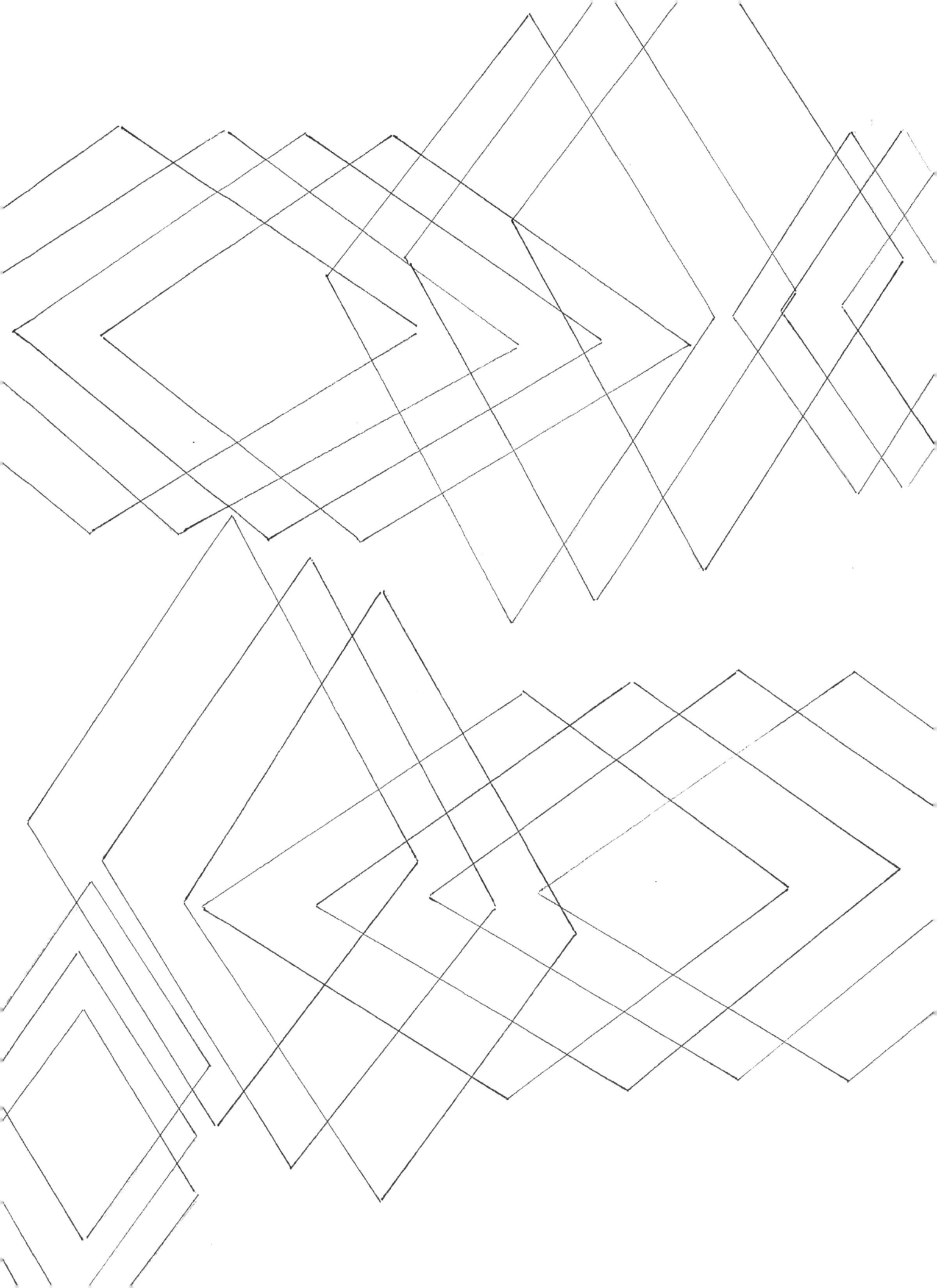

Journaling gives you the power of perspective.

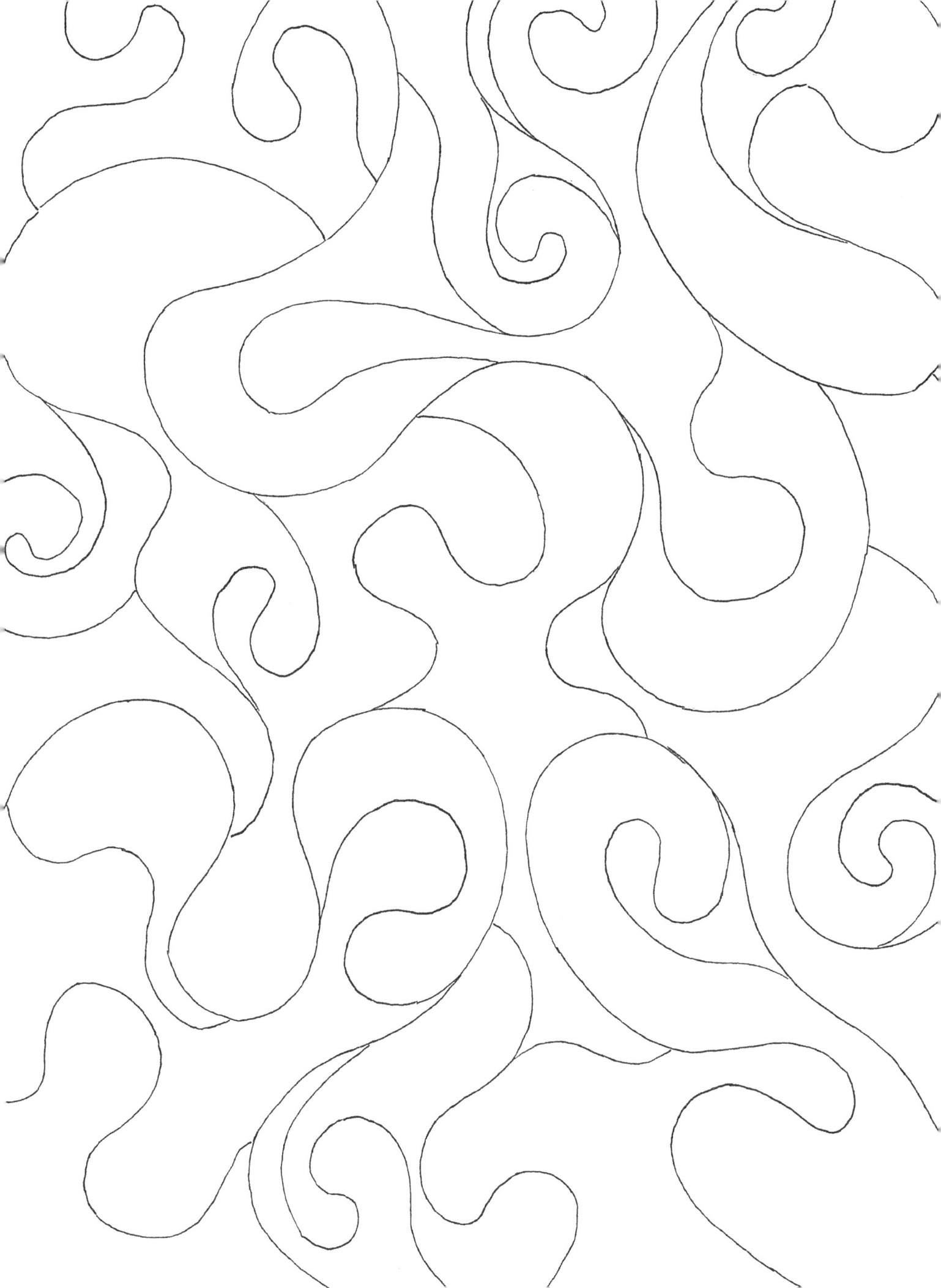

Journaling builds self-confidence.

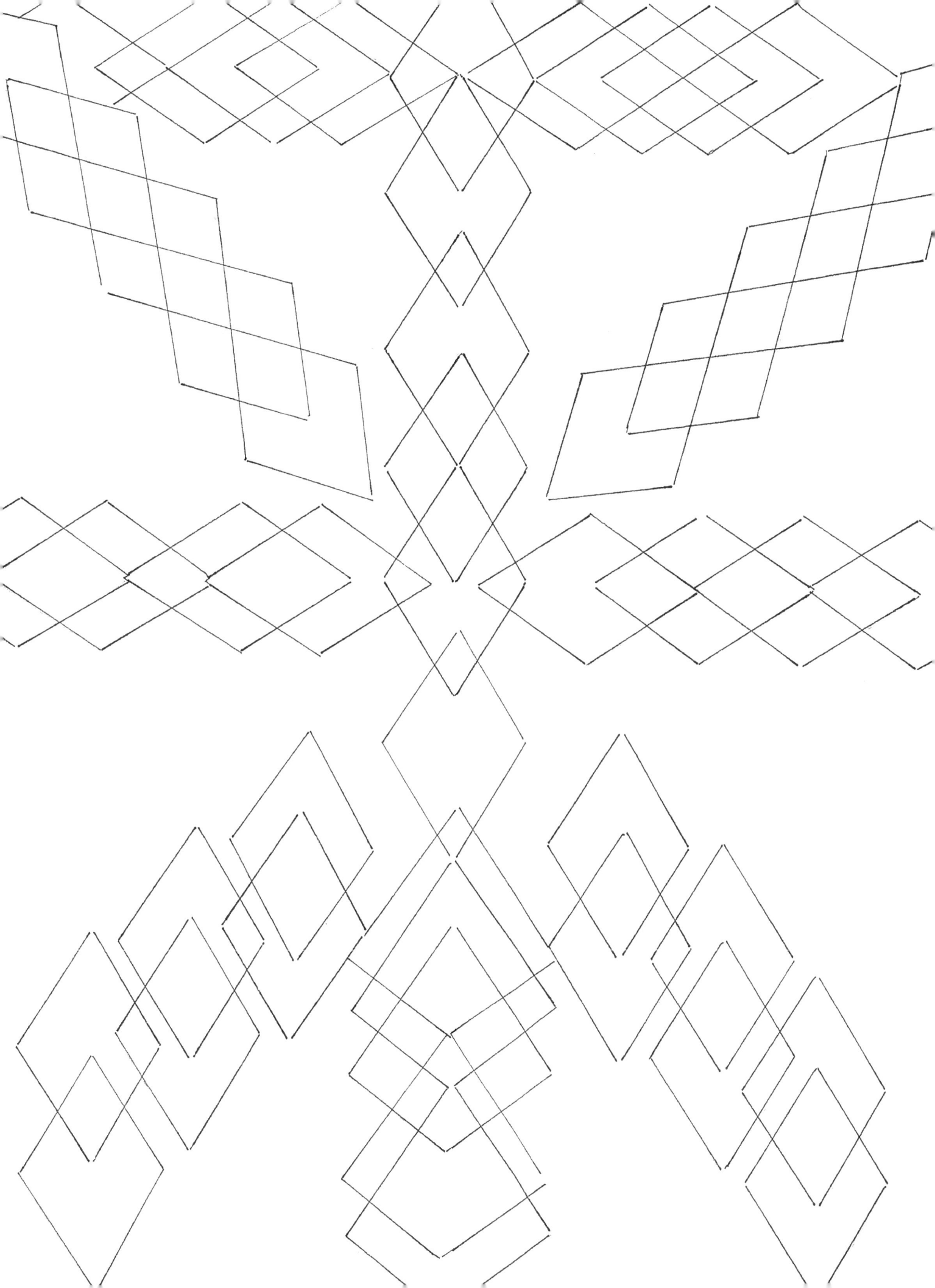

Journaling helps you notice your feelings, often an early indicator of something brewing.

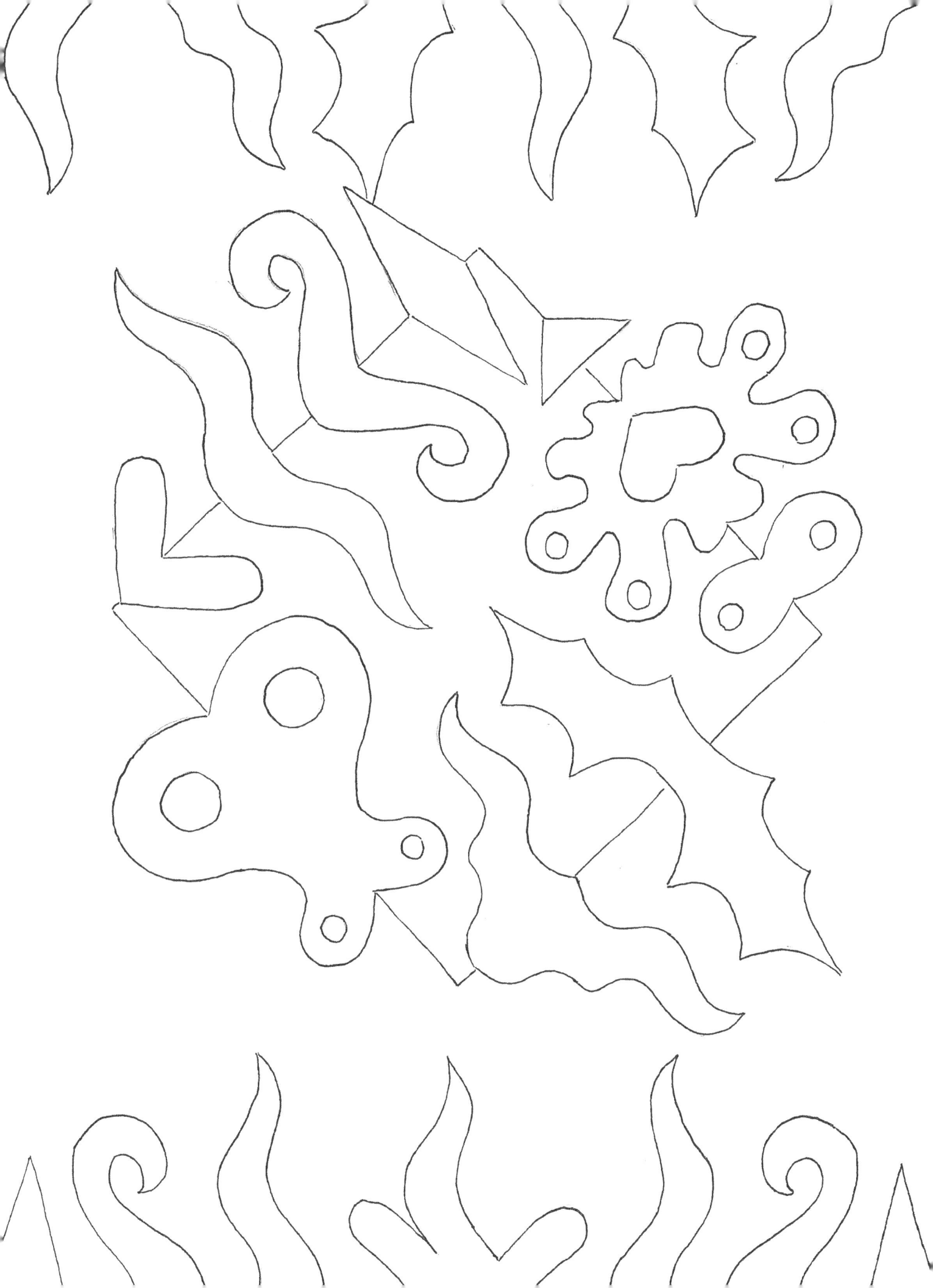

Journaling is a practice that teaches us the elusive art of solitude.

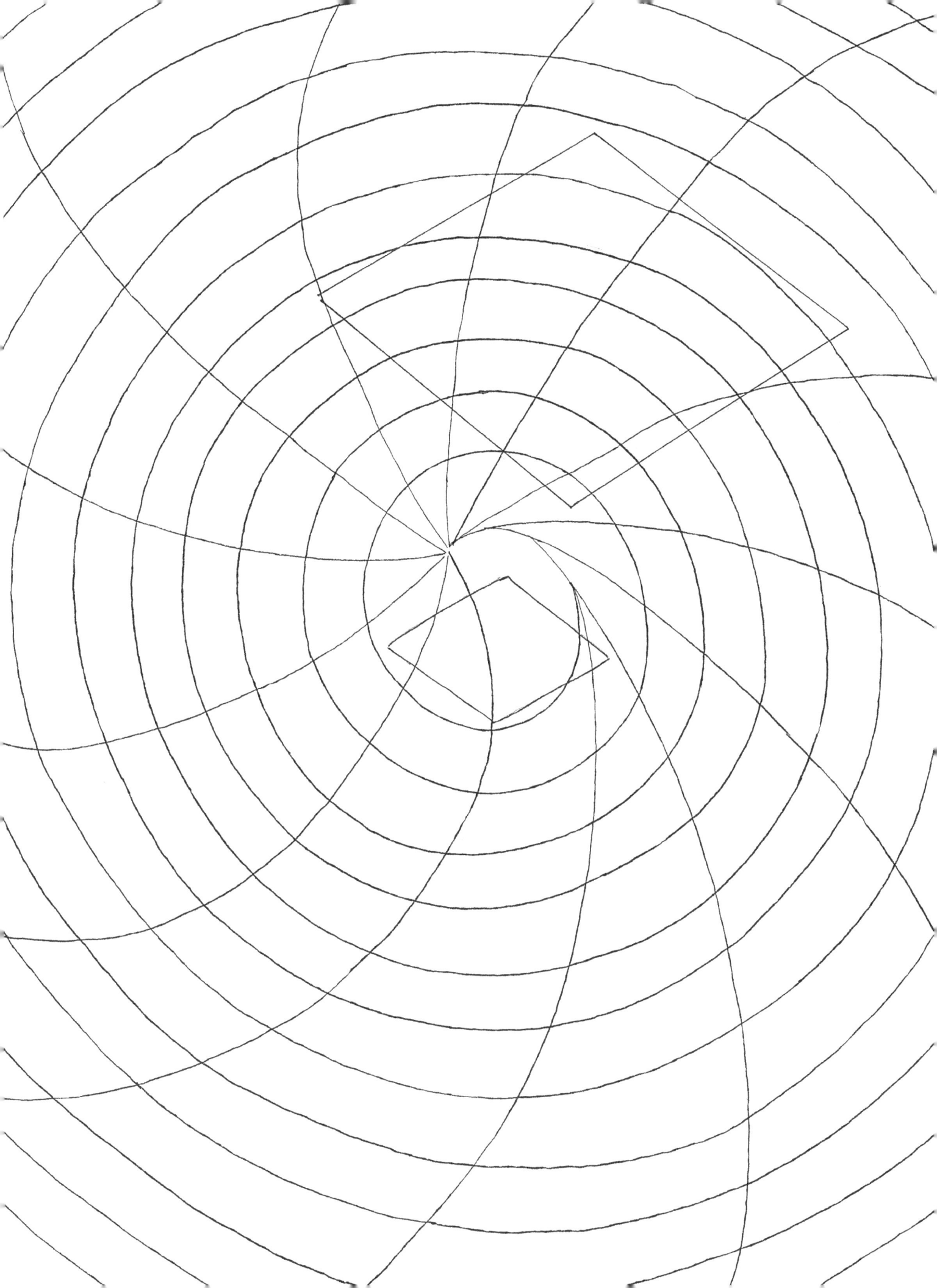

The act of journaling makes something more real than just thinking about it.

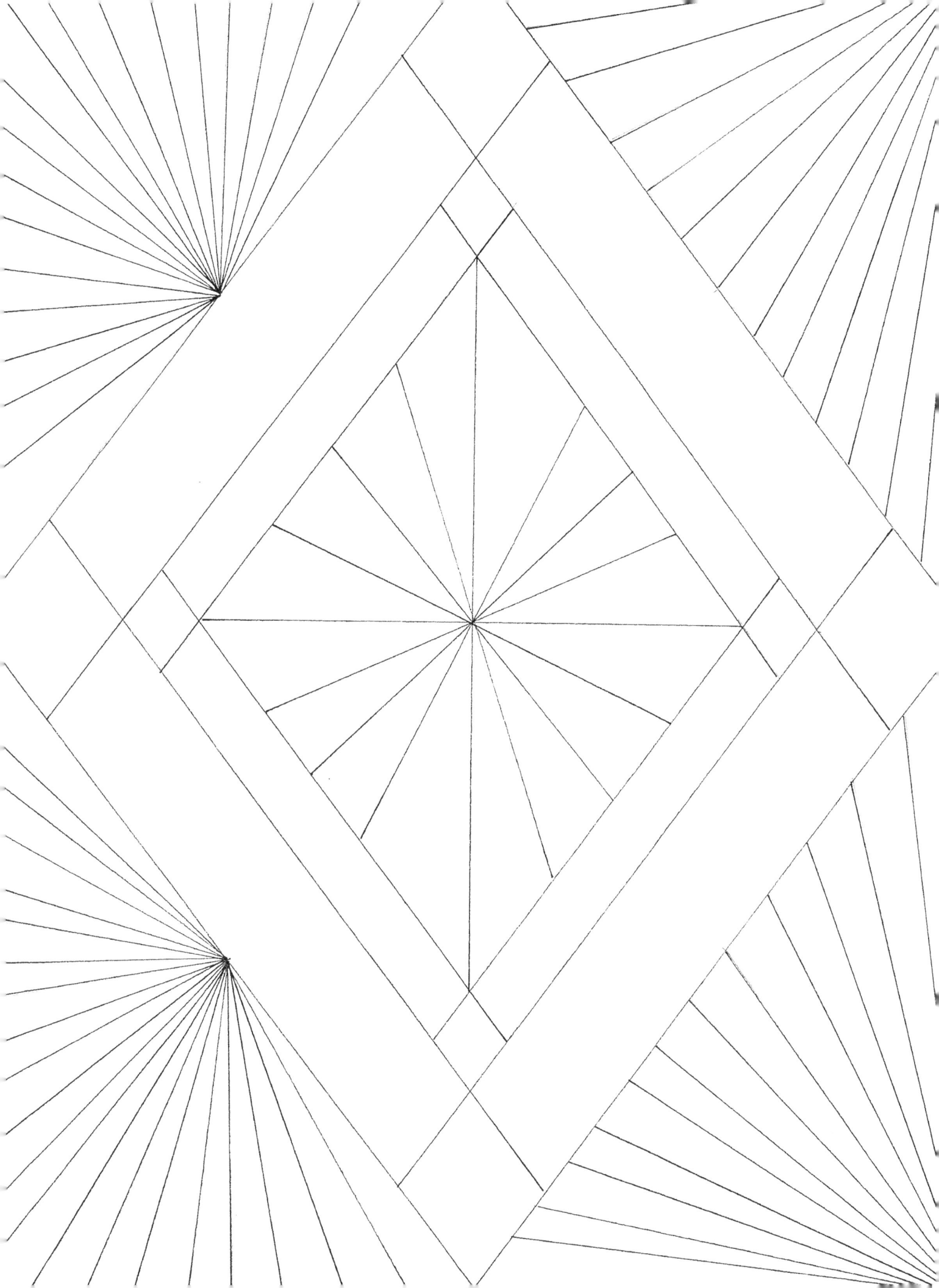

Your journal can have the potential to be both a therapist and a dear friend.

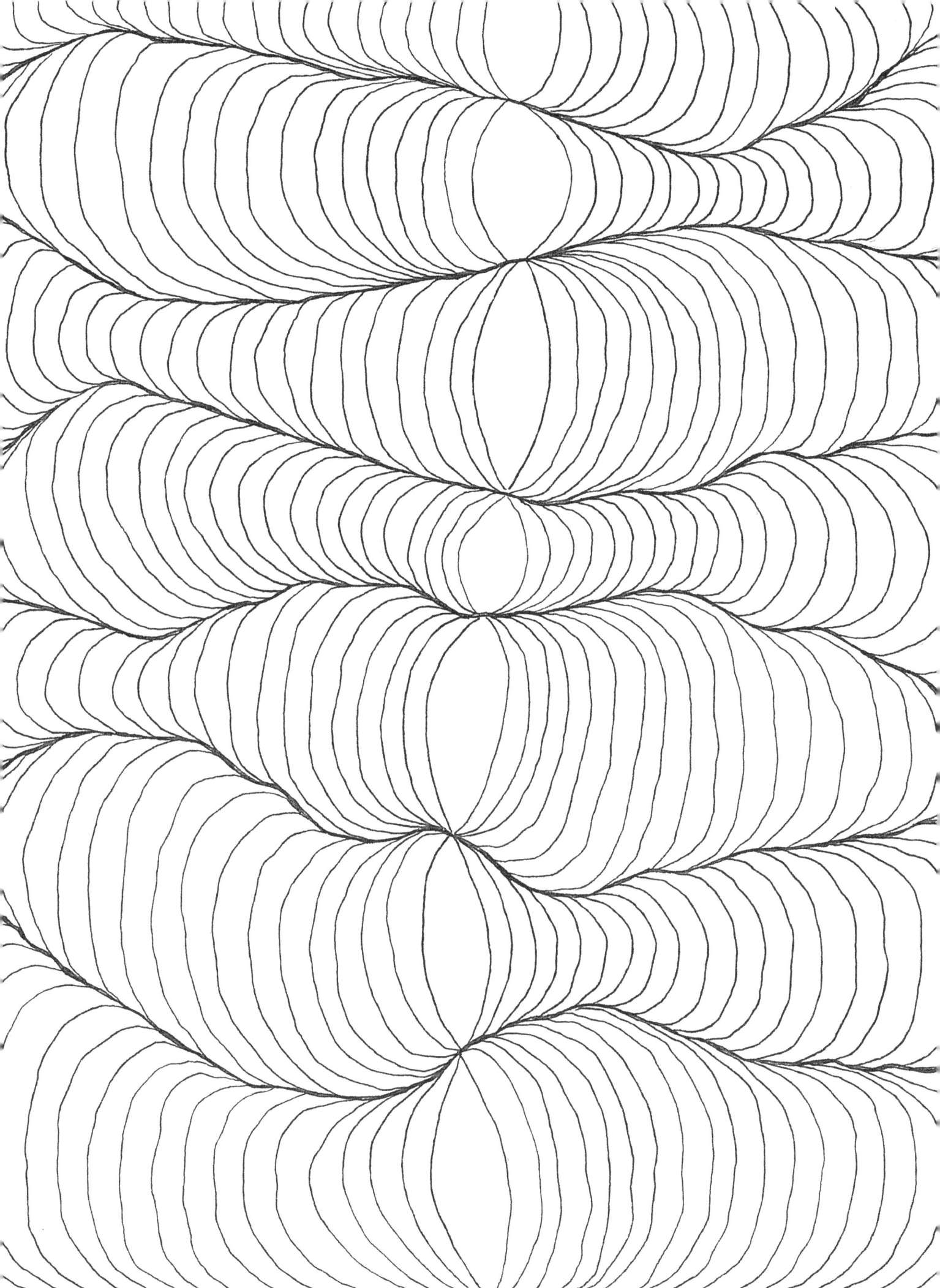

A journal is a precious treasure, especially the more it gets filled up.

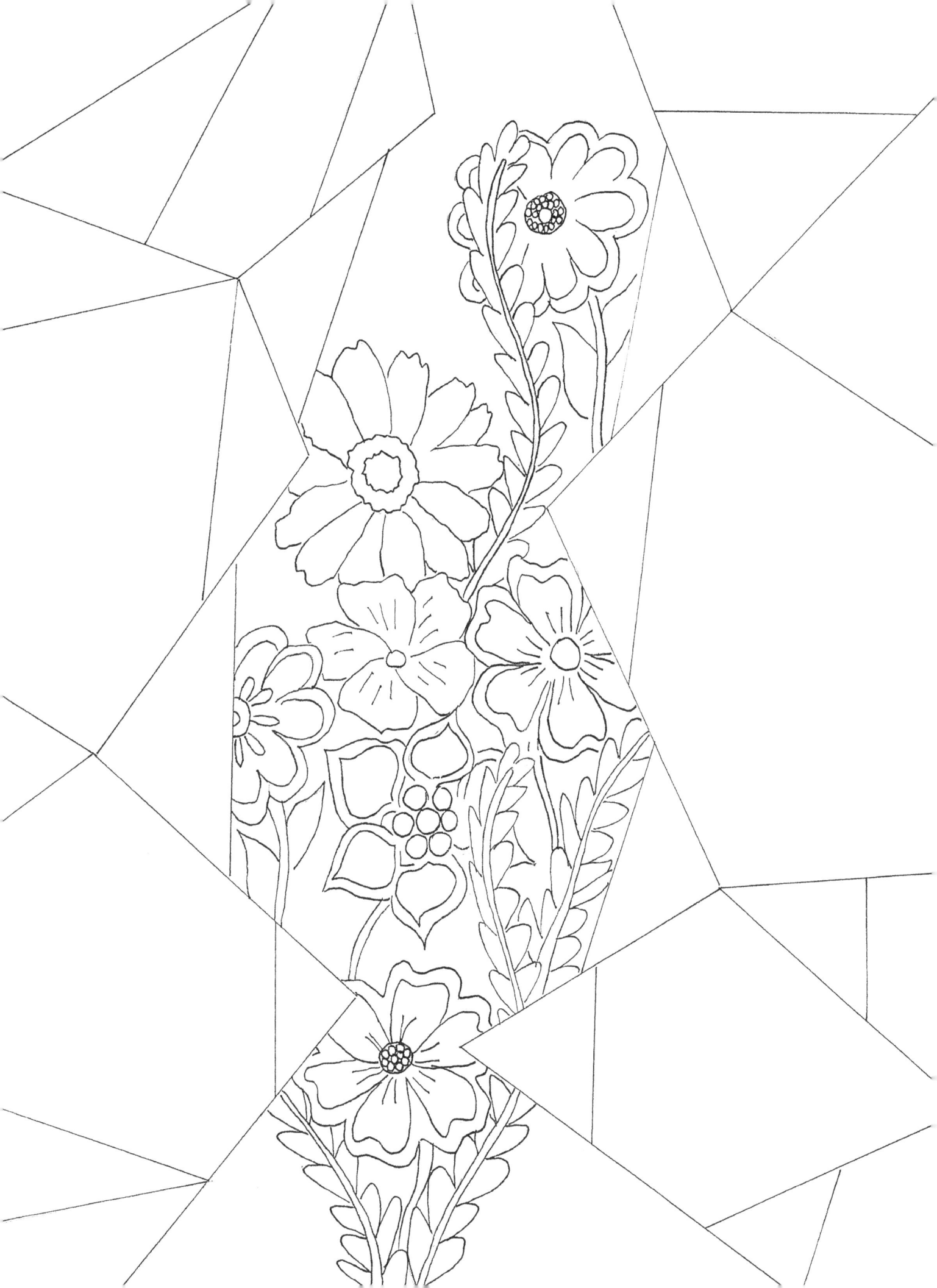

Blogging is a great way to get the benefits of journaling.

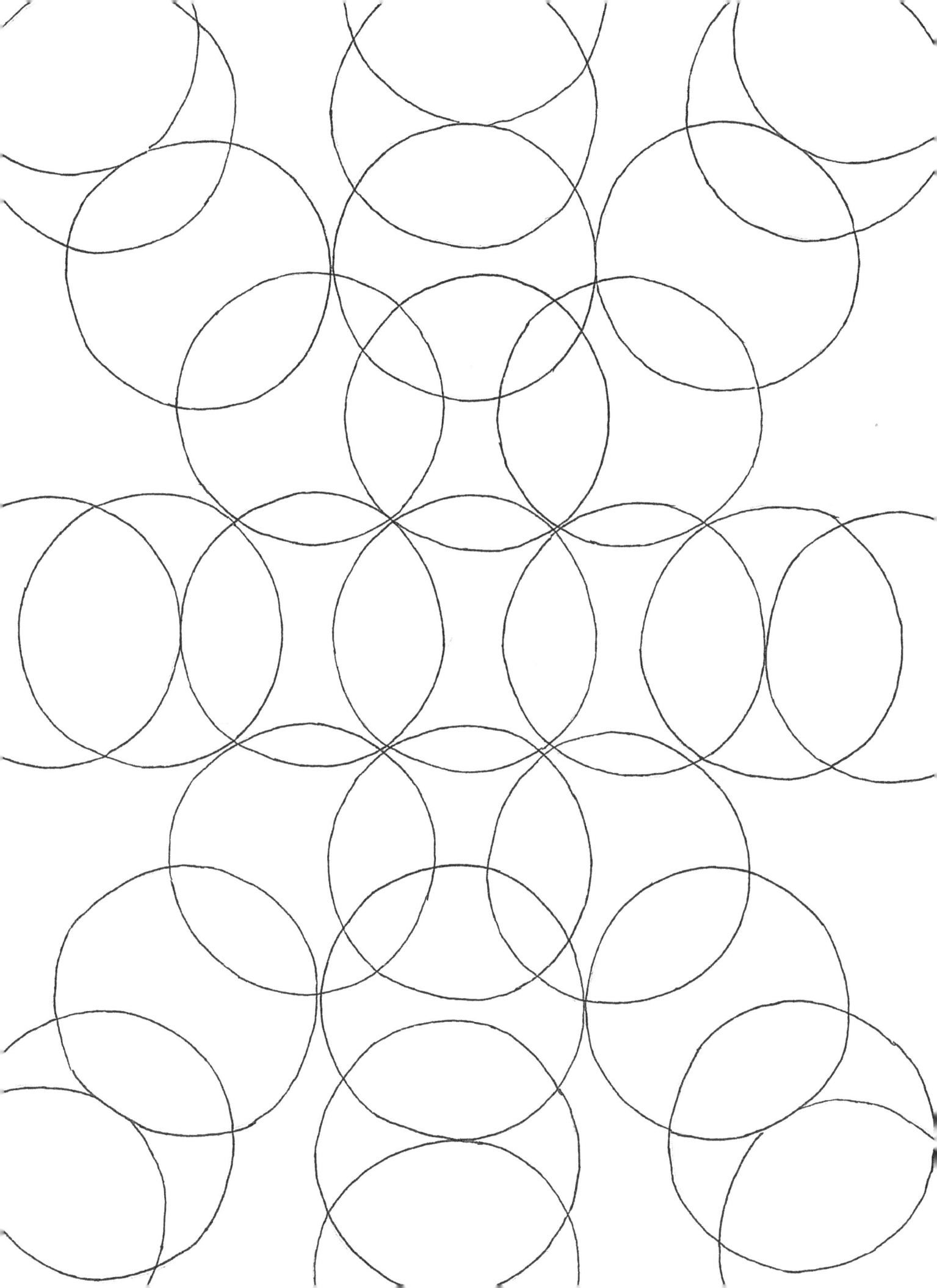

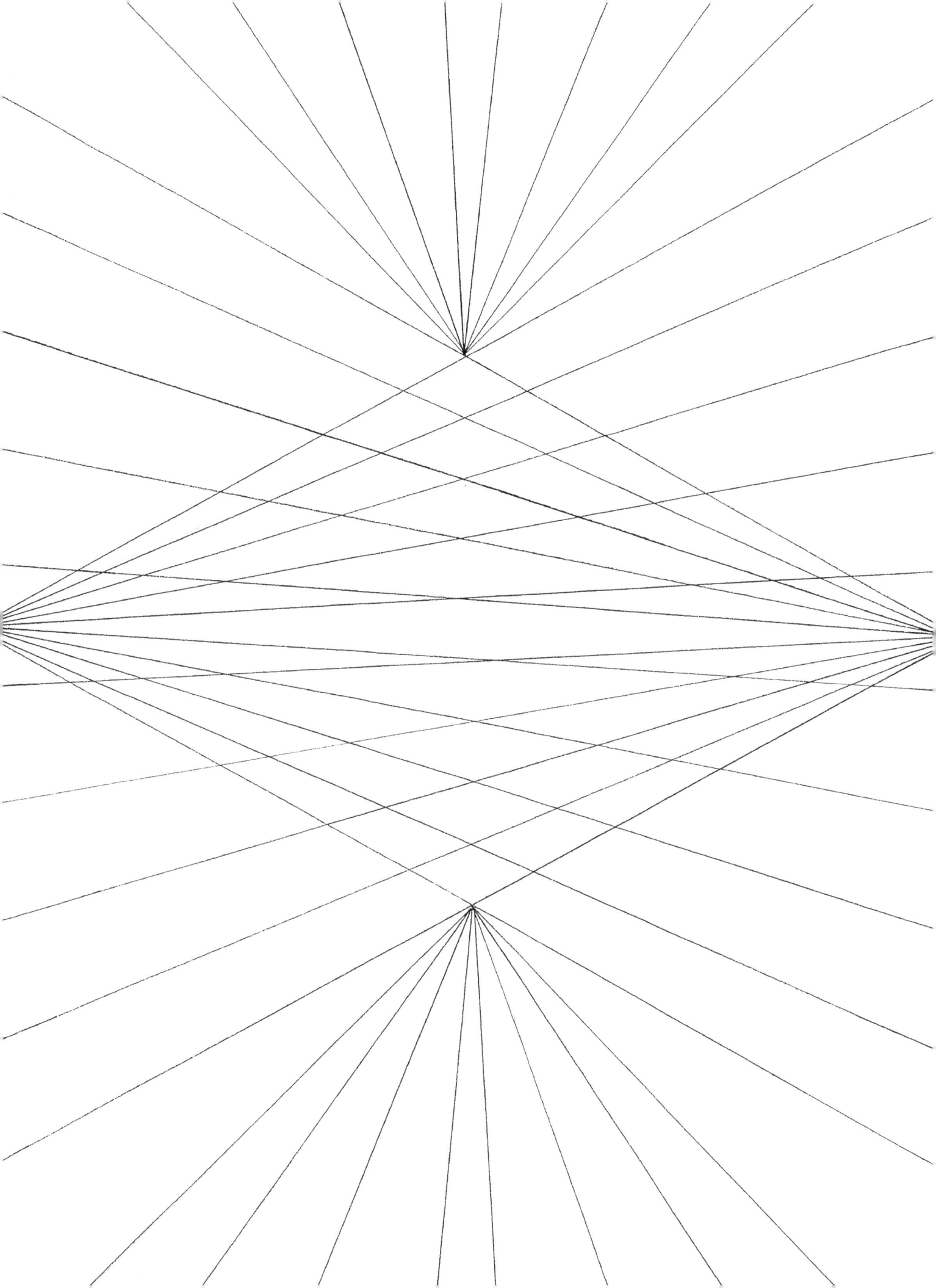

Journaling helps us reflect on thoughts we have as well as put them in some kind of order so that you can experience 'mastery' of situations.

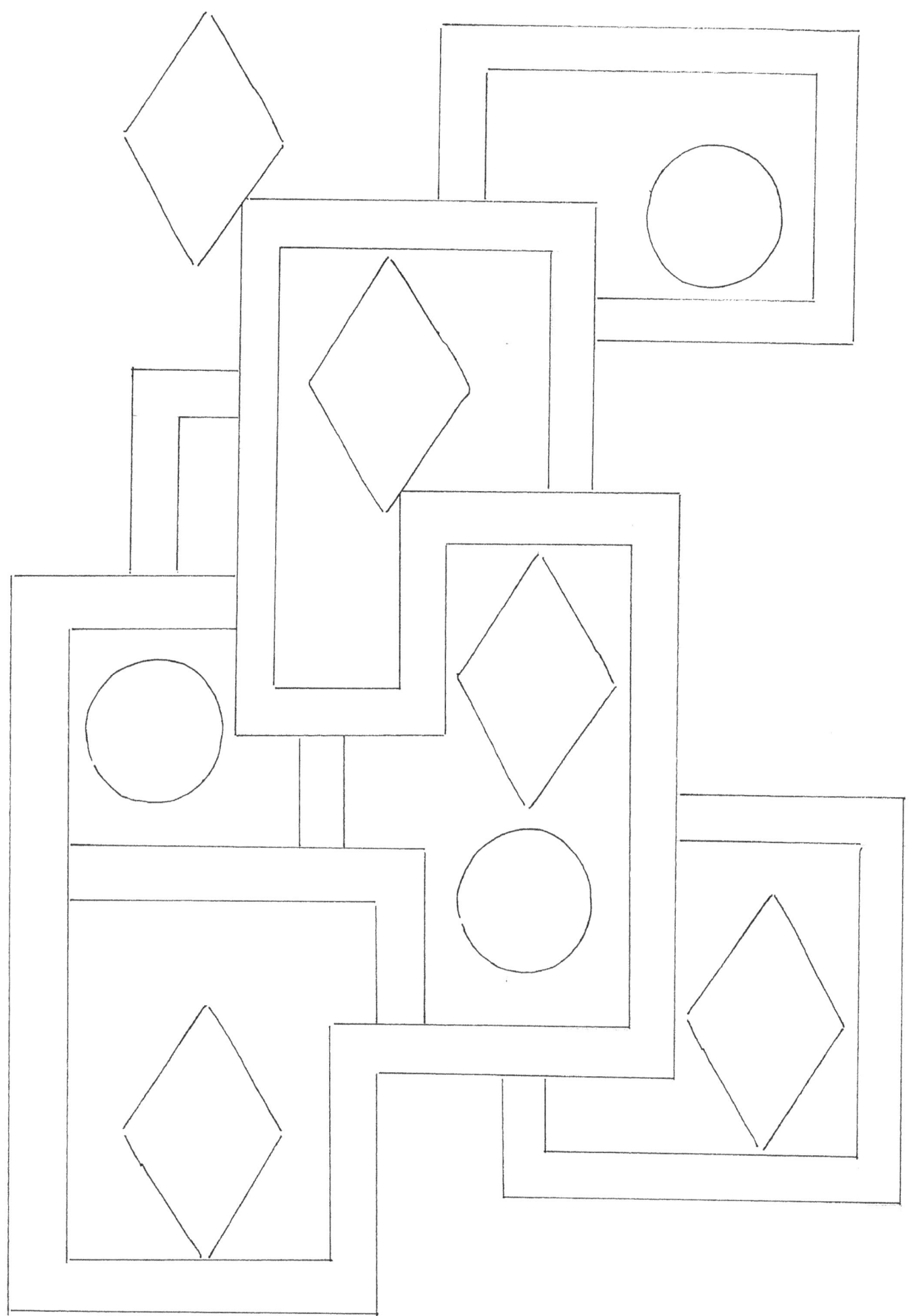

Give yourself some well-deserved moments of reflection from journaling.

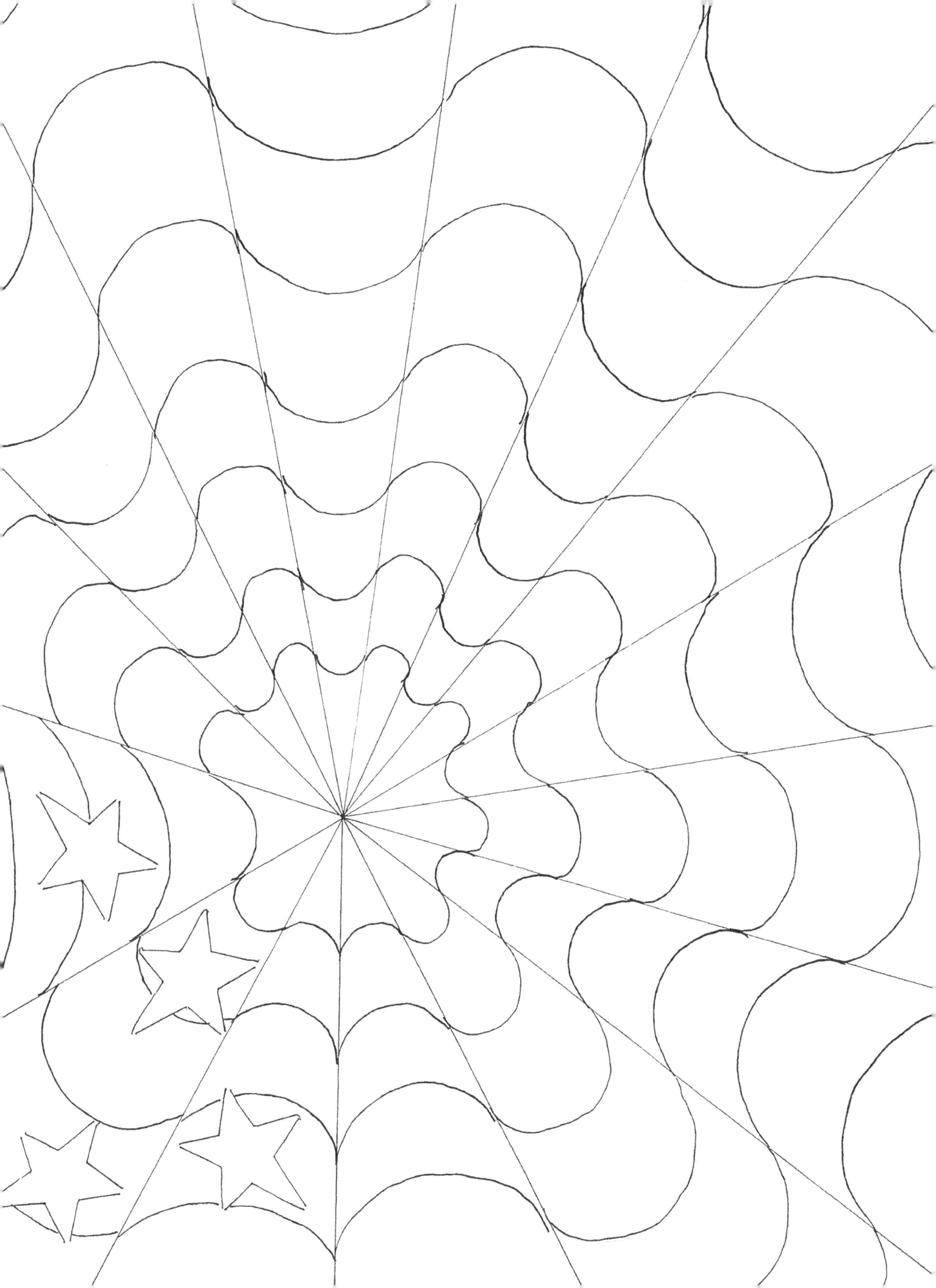

Clear your mind by writing in your journal.

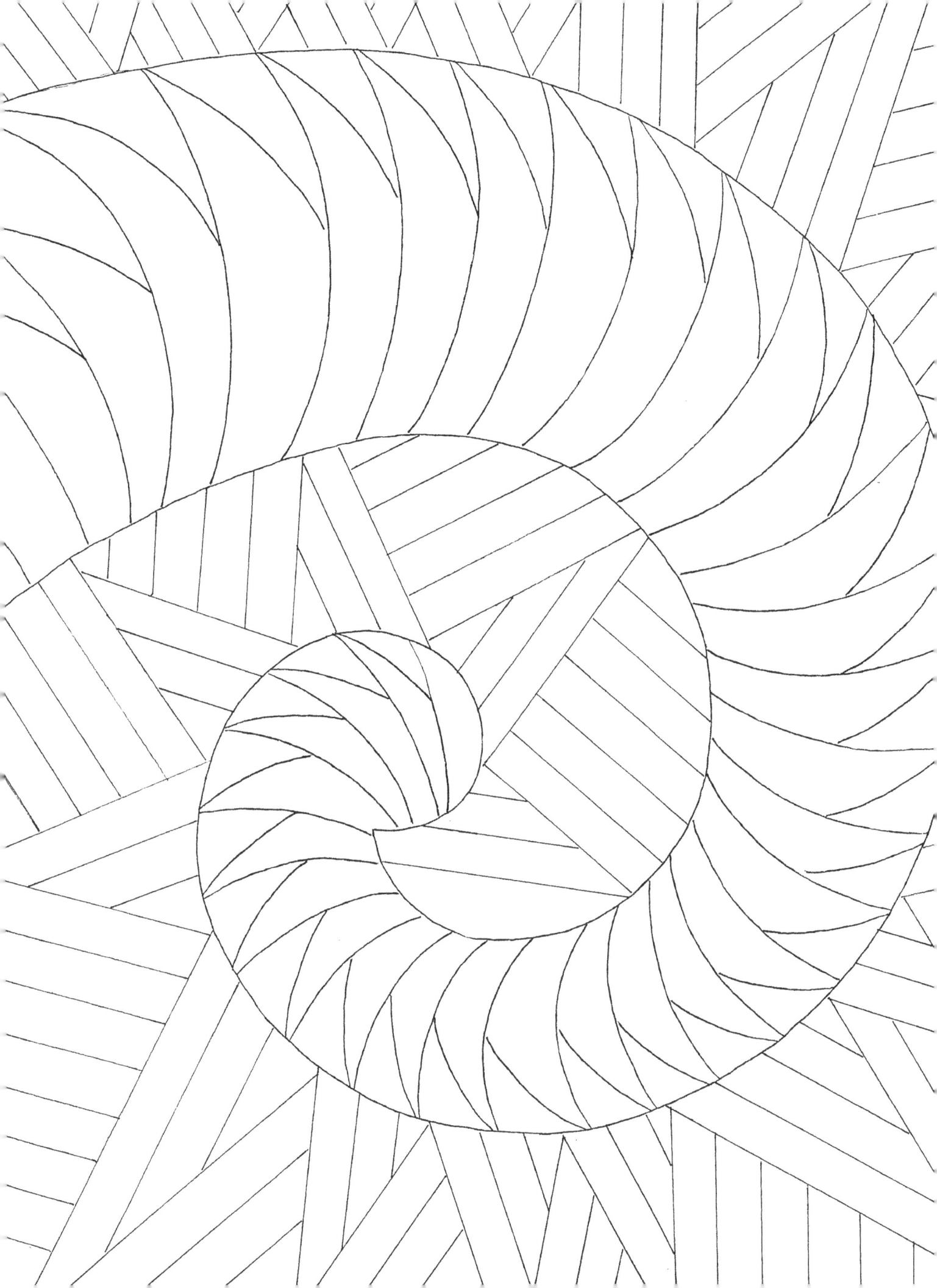

A unique sense of accomplishment comes from journaling.

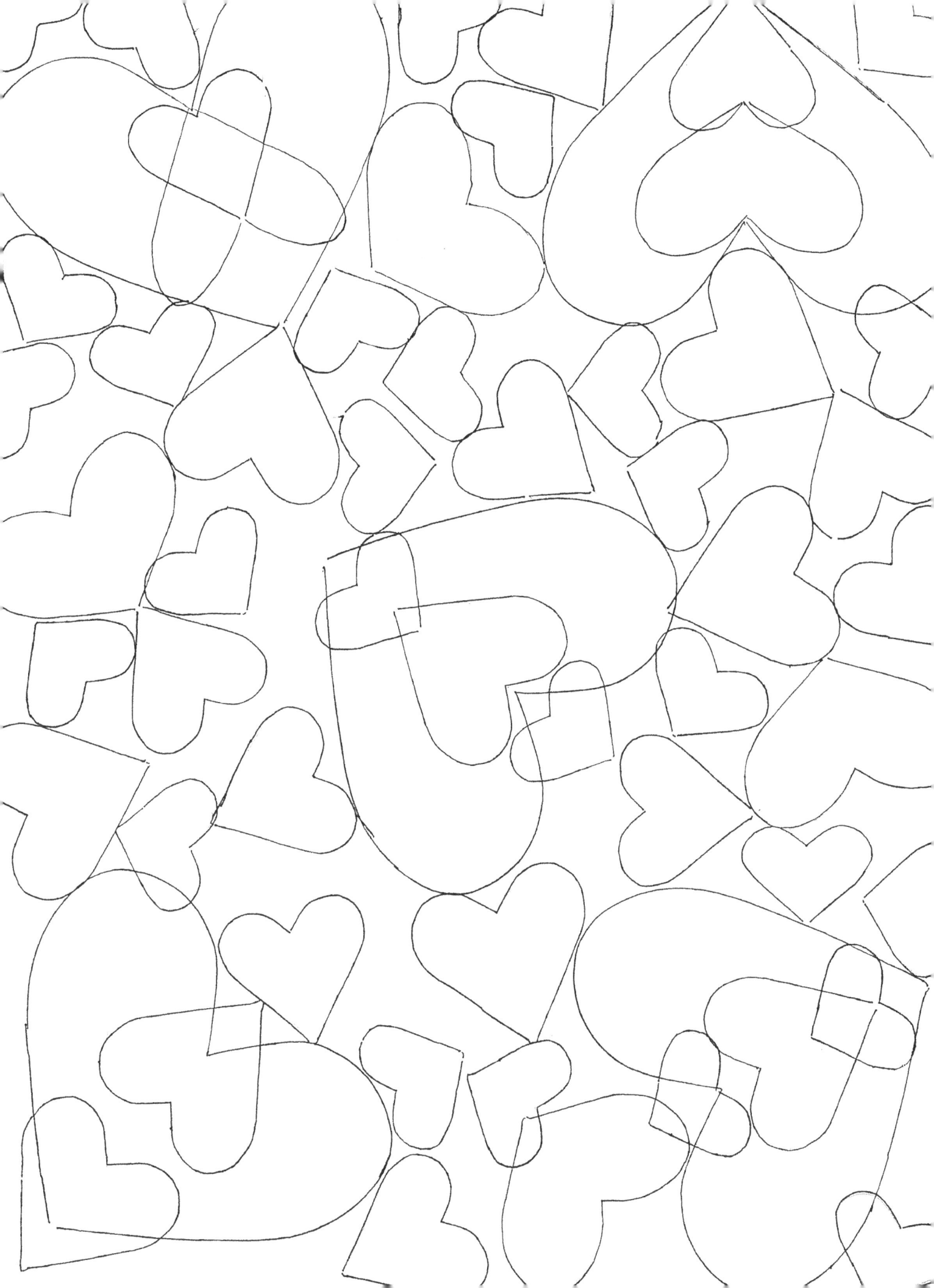

Record where you have come from, where you are now, and where you are going in your journal.

Capture ideas in your journal.

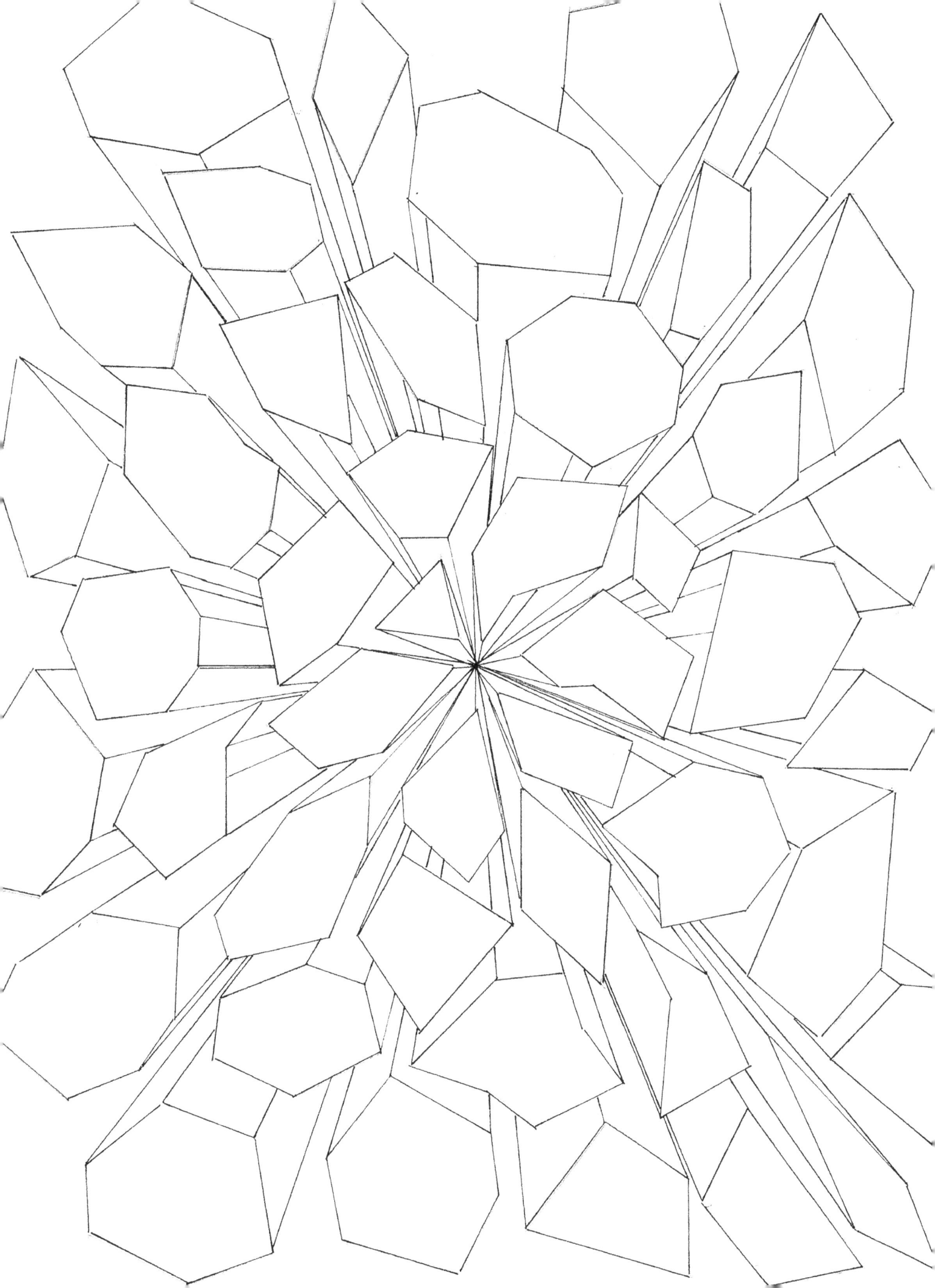

Find your inner peace and calm from writing your thoughts and coloring.

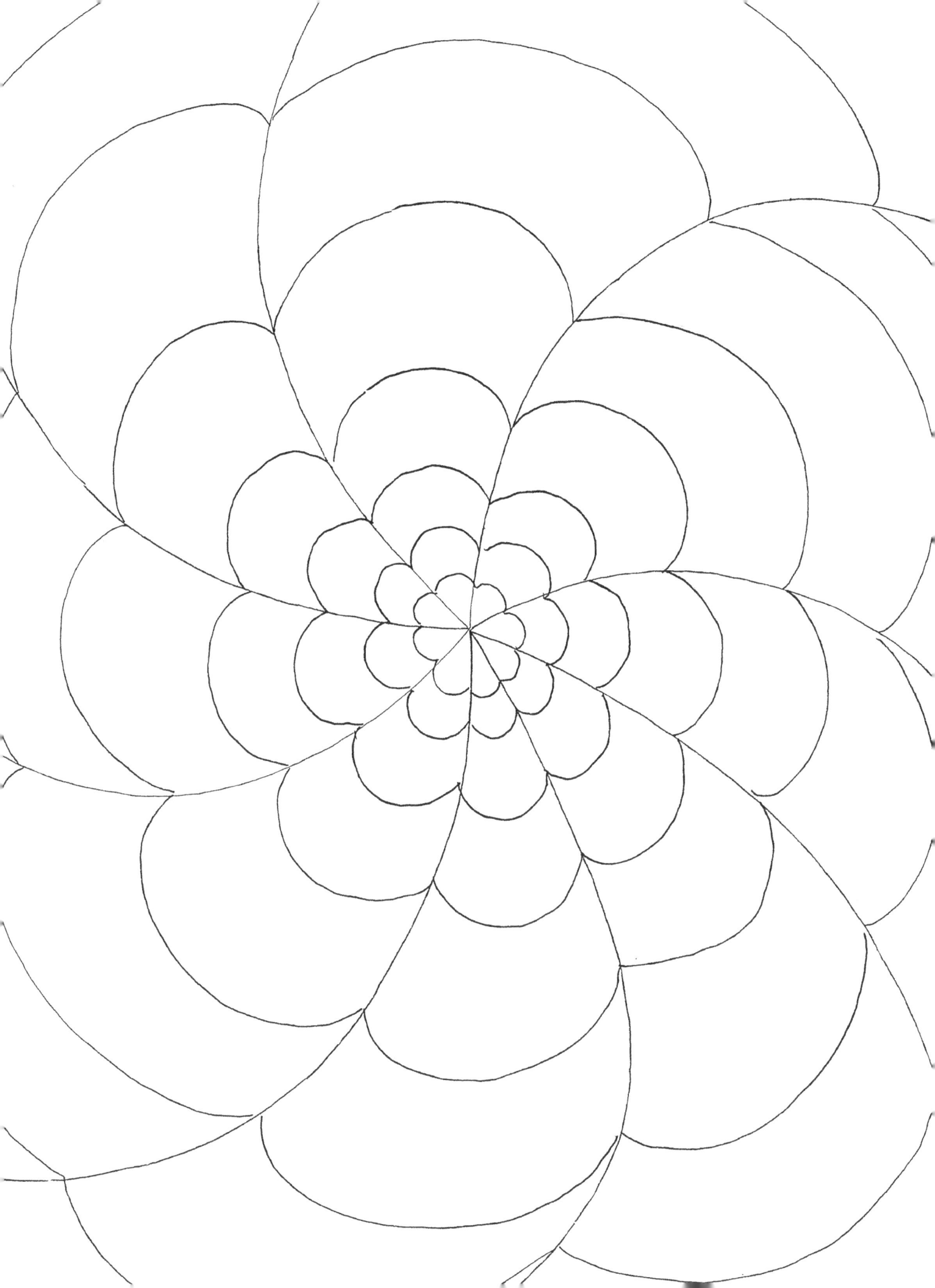

Journaling provides clear communication and offers the utmost in personal expression.

www.ingramcontent.com/pod-product-compliance
Lightning Source LLC
Chambersburg PA
CBHW080643190526
45169CB00009B/3485